Dehydrated Meals At Home and on the Go

By ML Flores
©2015

This is for those of you who want to prep for the future, want to go on a camping or back packing trip and those who are just on a tight income. These are light weight don't take up a lot of room and if you invest in a vacuum sealer they will last for a very long time. I have include a few breakfast lunch and dinner ideas that will sustain you in any given situation. Enjoy and remember to always rotate your stock.

Breakfast

Instant Oatmeal

Instant Grits

Pancake Mix

Ramen Noodle Ideas

Beef Noodles

Vege Ramen

Tomato Ramen

Sour Cream Ramen

Bean & Vege Ramen

Ramen & Kraut

Cheesy Rama

Seafood Rainer

Ham & Pea

Box Meals Turned MRE

Beef Stroganoff

Lucky's Stroganoff

Lasagna

Herb Chicken

Spanish rice

Red Beans & Rice

Couscous with Beef & Tomato

Macaroni & Cheese Ideas

Ham & Cheese Macaroni

Kickin' Mac & Cheese

Taco Mac & Cheese

Instant Oatmeal and Grits

Breakfast

Instant oatmeal and Grits.

Go to your local grocery and buy your favorite kind of Instant oatmeal or Instant grits. Buy some dry milk if you like milk in your oatmeal. If not the no worries. Add 2 tablespoons of dried milk to your oatmeal or grits then add you hot water. Allow it to sit for a few minutes then eat up and enjoy. It's a quick and easy meal.

Pre made Pancake Mix and Waffle Mix

5 cups plain flour

3 tbsp. baking powder

2tsp baking soda

1 tsp salt

3 tbsp. sugar

Storage

Place in an airtight container and leave in the pantry until you wish to use it

Prep

1 cup pre-made pancake mix

1 egg (optional)

1 1/2 cup milk (optional-water replacement)

1 tbsp. melted butter (optional)

Place 1 cup of mixture into a bowl

Add egg, milk & melted butter and mix

Cook each side in a frypan/griddle until golden.

I have a lot of the ingredients marked as optional. They are optional because if you don't have them you can still make this recipe without them. They may not be as fluffy or taste as good but in a survival situation food will be just that, food.

There are a lot of things you can do for breakfast but only a few can be dehydrated and made light weight. I have canned bacon, ham, potatoes and omelets but because they ae canned and not dried they have a little more weight to them. I tried to can bread and while it was great with the portion control it is not something I would recommend canning unless you plan on using it quickly.

You can also buy rolled oats and Grits in their natural form and cook them at home and then dehydrate them which would make them instant. That way you can add whatever you want to the recipe and measure out you portions to suit your needs.

Rolled Oats Bark

½ Cup rolled oat

1 apple or banana cut into pieces (optional)

1 Tbsp. raisins, cranberries (optional)

1 Tbsp. Maple syrup, honey or brown sugar

½ tsp Cinnamon

Pinch Salt

1 Cup water

1/4 teaspoon lemon juice

Prep:

Combine all ingredients in pot and bring to boil for two minutes. Reduce heat to simmer for five minutes and then turn off stove. Let pot sit covered for ten minutes.

Allow oatmeal to cool and then run through a blender until smooth.

Spread thinly on dehydrator tray covered with non-stick sheet.

Dehydrate at 135° F for approximately eight hours.

After six hours, the bark should be dry enough to flip over and finish drying without the non-stick sheet.

Break dried oat bark into pieces and store in a jar with tight fitting lid until ready to pack.

This recipe yields 1½ cups of oat bark which would be one large serving of oatmeal or it can be divided up and added to trail mix recipes.

If desired, you can be turn it back into oatmeal on the trail with an equal amount of boiled water and a little vigorous stirring.

Lunch or Dinner

Ginger Beef Noodles

4 tablespoons shredded beef jerky

1 3-ounce package ramen noodles

1 1-ounce package instant onion soup

2 tablespoon mixed dehydrated vegetables

1/4 teaspoon crushed red pepper

1/4 teaspoon garlic powder

¼ teaspoon onion powder

1/4 teaspoon ground ginger

1/2 teaspoon dried cilantro

1-2 packets soy sauce

Directions

Boil 2 cups of water. Add water to bag and stir. Let noodles soften and vegetables rehydrate for about 5 minutes. Season with soy sauce to taste

Vege Ramen

One package ramen, broken up to take up less space
(Don't use the flavor packet)

1 tablespoon each dried-

green pepper

red pepper

green beans

carrots

celery

potatoes

(You can buy boxes of sliced potatoes with au gratin or sour cream and onion flavorings at any grocery store. Save the flavor packets for other recipes.)

1 teaspoon onion flakes

1/8 teaspoon granulated garlic

salt & pepper to taste

1/4 teaspoon of chili powder or curry powder if you like it spicy (optional)

a tablespoon of dried mushrooms, dried peas, dried corn, or other dried
vegetables of your choice (optional)

Combinations:

Tomato Vegetable Ramen - Vege Ramen with the following changes:

1/2 can tomato sauce leather

add oregano, rosemary, thyme, basil, black pepper, garlic and onion powder, chili powder

Sour Cream Ramen - Vegetable Ramen with the following changes:

1/8 cup sour cream and chive mix from boxed potato meal

Beans & Ramen Noodles

½ Cup ramen noodles

¼ Cup home dried black beans

¼ Cup dried vegetables

¼ cup home dried white beans

green beans

tomatoes

corn

onions

celery

½ Cube vegetarian bouillon

1 Cup water

Combine all ingredients with one cup water and soak for five minutes.

Light stove, bring to boil, and continue cooking for one minute.

Let steep for about 10 minutes.

Ramen and Kraut

½ Cup ramen noodles

¼ Cup dried mixed vegetables

¼ Cup dried ground turkey, chicken or pork

2 Tbsp. dried sauerkraut

1 Cup water

Use fresh sauerkraut found in the refrigerated section of your grocery store next to the sausage.

Dehydrate at 125° for approximately four to six hours until crispy.

Pack all dry ingredients in a 4 x 6 plastic bag.

On the Trail:

Follow same cooking procedure as Vege Ramen Noodles.

Cheeseburger Vege Mac

½ Cup ramen noodles

¼ Cup dried meat

¼ Cup dried mixed vegetables

1 Tbsp. + 1 tsp cheddar cheese powder

1 Tbsp. powdered milk

Pinch crushed red pepper

1 Cup water

Combine and pack cheese powder and milk powder in a 2 x 3 plastic bag and enclose with other ingredients in a 4 x 6 plastic bag. Use the cheese powder from boxes of macaroni and cheese. For milk powder, use whole dry milk.

On the Trail:

Combine all ingredients except the cheese and milk powder in pot with one cup water and soak for five minutes.

Light stove, bring to a boil, and continue cooking for another minute.

Remove pot from stove, add cheese and milk power, and stir vigorously.

Cover pot and steep for ten minutes.

Seafood Rainer

½ Cup ramen noodles (half package)

¼ Cup dried shrimp and/or crabmeat

¼ Cup dried vegetables –

peppers

onions

mushrooms

tomatoes

¼ Cup tomato sauce leather, tightly packed

2 Tbsp. parmesan cheese

1 Cup water

Break noodles into small pieces. Pack parmesan cheese and tomato sauce leather separately in small plastic bags. Enclose in a larger plastic bag with noodles, seafood, and vegetables.

On the Trail:

Combine all ingredients except parmesan cheese with water in pot and soak for five minutes.

Light stove, bring to a boil, and continue cooking with the lid on for one minute.

Remove pot from stove and wait ten minutes. Insulate pot if possible. Stir in parmesan cheese before serving.

Ham and Pea Ramen

1-2 packages Ramen noodles

1/2 cup dried sweet peas

Parmesan cheese

Ham

Red pepper flakes

At home: Repack Ramen noodles and dried peas into one zip lock bag, throwing away the flavor packs. In another zip lock bag combine cheese, ham, salt and pepper to taste.

On the trail: Add noodles and peas to a pot of boiling water. Once cooking, drain the water. Mix in cheese, ham, and red pepper.

Beef Stroganoff

½ Cup noodles

¼ Cup dehydrated ground beef

¼ Cup dehydrated vegetables-
peppers

onions

tomatoes

celery

potatoes

2 Tbsp. stroganoff sauce mix

1 Tbsp. powdered milk

1 Cup water

On the Trail:

Place all ingredients except sauce mix and powdered milk in pot with water and soak for five minutes.

Light stove, bring to boil, and continue cooking for another two minutes.

Remove pot from stove, stir in sauce mix and powdered milk, replace lid, steep for ten minutes.

Sauce thickens as it cools.

Lucky's Stroganoff Recipe

1 Cup homemade instant rice

½ package Beef Stroganoff Sauce Mix

2 Tbsp. oil

2 Tbsp. powdered sour cream

3 Tbsp. dried hamburger

3 Tbsp. dried mushrooms

On the Trail:

Bring 1¼ cups water to a boil. Remove pot from heat and stir in all ingredients. Steep for 10 minutes. Stir and enjoy!

Vegetarian Option:

Leave out the hamburger and double the mushrooms.

Lasagna

½ Cup noodles

- ¼ Cup dehydrated ground beef

- ¼ Cup dehydrated vegetables

tomatoes

mushrooms

onions

peppers

garlic

1½ Tbsp. sauce powder

1 - 2 Tbsp. parmesan cheese

1 Cup water

On the Trail:

Place all ingredients except tomato sauce mix and parmesan cheese in pot with water and soak for five minutes.

Light stove, bring to boil, and continue cooking for another two minutes.

Remove pot from stove, stir in tomato sauce mix, replace lid, and steep for ten minutes.
After removing lid, sauce will thicken as it cools. Top with parmesan cheese. Enjoy!

Cheddar Herb Chicken

½ Cup penne pasta

¼ Cup dehydrated ground or canned chicken

¼ Cup dehydrated green beans or broccoli
(vegetable of choice)

1 Tbsp. + 1 tsp cheddar herb sauce mix

1 Tbsp. powdered milk

1 Cup water

At Home:

Pack sauce mix and powdered milk in a 2 x 3 plastic bag.
Enclose with other ingredients in a 4 x 6 plastic bag.

On the Trail:

Place all ingredients except cheddar herb sauce mix and powdered milk in pot with water and soak five minutes.

Light stove, bring to boil, and continue cooking for another two minutes. If you have plenty of fuel, three minutes of boiling wouldn't hurt since the noodles are thicker than other boxed noodle products.

Remove pot from stove, stir in sauce mix and powdered milk, replace lid, steep for
ten minutes. Sauce thickens as it cools.

Spanish Rice

½ Cup rice and seasoning

¼ Cup dehydrated ground beef

¼ Cup dehydrated tomatoes (sliced cherry or diced)

1 Cup water

At Home:

You will need to add extra instant rice to get three servings out of the box. Fill a 1-cup measuring cup with Spanish Rice mixture. Next, add the remaining Spanish Rice mixture to a ½-cup measuring cup and then top off with added instant rice. Mix back in with the first cup. You now have 1½ cups of rice and seasoning which can be divided into three servings.

Pack all ingredients in a 4 x 6 plastic bag.

On the Trail:

Place all ingredients in pot with water and soak for five minutes.

Light stove, bring to boil, and continue cooking for two minutes.

Remove pot from stove and steep for ten minutes.

Red Beans and Rice

¾ Cup Zatarain's® Red Beans and Rice

¼ Cup dehydrated vegetables (garlic, celery, peppers, onions, tomatoes also try okra)

1¼ Cups water

Large Portion:

This recipe provides 413 calories. To make a larger portion with 506 calories, use 1 cup Zatarain's® Red Beans and Rice, ⅓ cup vegetables, and 1½ cups water to rehydrate.

On the Trail:

Place all ingredients in pot with water and soak for five minutes.

Light stove, bring to boil, and continue cooking for two minutes.

Remove pot from stove and steep for ten minutes.

Couscous with Beef & Tomato

½ box couscous (slightly less than ½ cup)

1 Tbsp. Near East® Seasoning Mix (half the pack)

¼ Cup dehydrated tomatoes (sliced cherry or diced)

¼ Cup dehydrated ground beef or ground turkey

1¼ Cups water

On the Trail:

Place all ingredients except seasoning mix in pot with water and soak five minutes. Couscous absorbs more water than other pastas. Be prepared to add a little extra water.

Light stove, bring to boil, and continue cooking for one minute. Add a little water if necessary. Watch to make sure that the couscous doesn't stick to the bottom of the pot.

Alternative trail cooking method:

If you pack the couscous separate from the other ingredients, you can bring the meat and vegetables to a boil first and then add the couscous for one minute boiling time. This cooking method makes it less likely that couscous will stick to the bottom of the pot.

Remove pot from stove, stir in seasoning mix, replace lid, steep for ten minutes.

Ham and Cheese Macaroni

¼ Cup deli ham, dried

¼ Cup dried mixed vegetables-
peppers

corn

carrots

peas

green beans

½ cup macaroni

1 Tbsp. + 1 tsp cheddar cheese powder

1 Tbsp. powdered milk

1¼ Cups water

On the Trail:

Add all ingredients except the cheese/milk powder to your pot
with water. Allow contents to rehydrate for five minutes.

Light stove, bring to a boil, and continue cooking with the lid on
for two minutes.

Stir in cheese/milk powder, put the lid back on. Wait ten minutes
for the meal to continue rehydrating and steeping.

Kickin' Veggie Macaroni and Cheese

¼ Cup dried cherry tomato quarters or diced tomatoes

¼ Cup dried mixed peppers, onions, mushrooms

¼ teaspoon garlic granules

2 slices dried jalapeno peppers

Sprinkle in some chili powder

Pinch red pepper

½ Cup macaroni

1 Tbsp. + 1 tsp cheddar cheese powder

1 Tbsp. powdered milk

½ tsp taco seasoning

1¼ Cups water

On the Trail:

Add all ingredients except the cheese/milk/taco seasoning to your pot with water. Allow contents to rehydrate for five minutes.

Light stove, bring to a boil, and continue cooking with the lid on for two minutes.

Stir in cheese/milk/taco powder mix, put the lid back on, steep for 10 minutes.

Taco Mac and Cheese

¼ Cup ground beef, dried

¼ Cup mixed vegetables, dried
bell peppers
tomatoes
onions
mushrooms

2 slices dried jalapeno peppers

½ Cup macaroni

1 Tbsp. + 1 tsp cheddar cheese powder

1 Tbsp. powdered milk

½ tsp taco seasoning

Pinch red pepper

1¼ Cups water

On the Trail:

Add all ingredients except the cheese/milk mix/taco seasoning to your pot with water. Allow contents to rehydrate for five minutes.

Light stove, bring to a boil, and continue cooking with the lid on for two minutes.

Stir in contents of the cheese/milk/taco powder mix, put the lid back on, and place pot into insulating cozy. Wait ten minutes for the meal to continue rehydrating and cooking inside the cozy.

Mock Stuffed Pepper Soup

¼ cup homemade instant rice

¼ cup dehydrated green bell peppers

¼ cup dehydrated red bell peppers

¼ cup dehydrated orange bell peppers

¼ cup dehydrated ground beef

¼ cup dehydrated tomato sauce leather

oregano, pinch

thyme, pinch

Italian seasoning, pinch

pinch of basil

dash of hot sauce

3 cups water to rehydrate

garlic, onion, salt and pepper powder to taste

On the Trail:

Rehydrate with about three cups of water. Add seasonings, and pepper sauce to taste.

Bark Recipes

White/Red Potato Bark

2½ lbs. potatoes

16 ounces fat free vegetable, beef or chicken broth

Salt and Pepper to taste

Garlic/Onion Powder to taste(optional)

Cook, Mash & Blend

Peel and boil 2½ pounds of potatoes until soft. Drain.

Mash potatoes with 16 ounces of fat free vegetable, beef, or chicken broth. Because fats and dairy products don't dehydrate well and can spoil, do not add any milk or butter. Add salt, if desired, but you'll get some sodium from the broth.

Run the mashed potatoes through a blender or mixer until creamy and lump-free.

Dry It

Cover dehydrator trays with non-stick sheets or parchment paper.

Pour a six inch puddle of potatoes onto the covered tray and spread thinly (about an eighth inch) with a spatula. 2½ pounds of mashed potatoes will take up five 15 x 15 trays.

Dehydrate at 135° for approximately eight hours until potatoes form a brittle sheet.

Flip It

If you have an Excalibur Dehydrator, use the "flip-trick" as follows to thoroughly dry the underside of the potato sheet: After about five hours of drying, place a dehydrator tray on top of the potato sheet and flip the two trays over so that the moister bottom side is facing up.

The dried sheet of potatoes will easily snap into Bark or crush down for tighter packing.

Yield: 2½ pounds of potatoes will dehydrate down to 5½ ounces and fill two cups when crushed.

Sweet Potato Bark

1 large or 2 small Sweet Potatoes (approx. 13 ounces before peeling)

½ cup Apple Juice

1 Tbsp Real Maple Syrup/ raw honey

1 tsp Cinnamon (may include nutmeg)

Cook It

Peel sweet potatoes and cut into chunks.

Boil until soft, drain, and mash.

Stir in apple juice, maple syrup, and cinnamon. If you like nutmeg, you may replace half of the cinnamon with nutmeg.

Blend It

Run the mashed sweet potatoes through a blender until creamy. If your blender struggles with the mixture, add a few more spoonful's of juice or water.

Dry It

Cover dehydrator trays with parchment paper, or the fruit leather inserts that came with your dehydrator.

Spread thinly and as evenly as possible on covered dehydrator trays. Shoot for an eighth inch thickness. The quantities in this recipe will cover one Excalibur Dehydrator tray.

Dehydrate at 135° for eight to ten hours. The sweet potatoes will form a sheet that may have cracks running through it.

Flip It

After about six hours of drying, peel the bark off the non-stick sheets and flip it over to expose the bottom side to more hot air for the remainder of the drying time. Place the bark directly on the mesh dehydrator trays without the non-stick sheets.

Depending on how long you dry it, the sweet potato sheet will either tear like fruit leather or break into bark. For snacking and short term use, you may prefer to dry it to the leather stage. If packing for a trip that will last more than a month, dry it longer to the snappy bark stage.

Yield:

One large or two small sweet potatoes (approx. 13 ounces before peeling) will yield approximately ¾ cup of bark and weigh 2½ ounces. Increase the ingredients proportionately for larger batches.

Bean Bark

Run a 28 ounce can of vegetarian baked beans or an equivalent quantity of homemade beans through a blender until creamy. Use all the liquids from the can. Avoid using baked bean products containing bacon or pork because fatty meats will not dehydrate well and may spoil.

Pour puddles of blended beans on dehydrator trays covered with parchment paper and spread thinly with a spatula. Twenty-eight ounces of blended beans takes up three 15 x 15 Excalibur Dehydrator trays.

Dry at 135° F for eight hours. Unlike Potato Bark, which dries into a sheet, Bean Bark dries like mud... full of cracks.

After about six hours or when the bark is dry enough to pull off the trays, flip it over to expose the moister bottom side to the hot air.

Yield: 28 ounces of beans will bark down to three cups weighing seven ounces.

Corn Bark

Run a 15 ounce can of creamed sweet corn through a blender to a smoothie-like consistency.

Spread thinly on dehydrator tray covered with parchment paper.

Dehydrate at 135° F for 10 hours until brittle.

Flip Trick: When the sheet of corn is substantially dry after about seven hours, place another dehydrator tray over it and flip the two trays over so that the Bark is now stuck to the bottom of the top tray. Peel sheet of corn away and remove the top tray. The moister bottom side of the Bark will now be facing up for more thorough drying.

The sheet of corn will break into pieces easily when dry.

Rolled Oats Bark

½ Cup rolled oat

1 apple or banana cut into pieces (optional)

1 Tbsp. raisins, cranberries (optional)

1 Tbsp. Maple syrup, honey or brown sugar

½ tsp Cinnamon

Pinch Salt

1 Cup water

1/4 teaspoon lemon juice

Prep:

Combine all ingredients in pot and bring to boil for two minutes. Reduce heat to simmer for five minutes and then turn off stove. Let pot sit covered for ten minutes.

Allow oatmeal to cool and then run through a blender until smooth.

Spread thinly on dehydrator tray covered with non-stick sheet.

Dehydrate at 135° F for approximately eight hours.

After six hours, the bark should be dry enough to flip over and finish drying without the non-stick sheet.

Tomato Bark/Leather

Start with your homemade tomato sauce recipe or buy a jar of Marinara Sauce. Run the tomato sauce through a blender to a smoothie-like consistency. Blending any chunks of tomatoes or other vegetables in the sauce thickens the sauce so it will make better leather.

A little olive oil in the ingredients won't cause early spoilage, but don't dry cheesy sauces like Vodka Sauce or Three-Cheese Sauce I saw on you tube where you can can those if you're making them from scratch..

Spread the sauce thinly on dehydrator trays covered with parchment paper, or the fruit-roll sheets that came with your dehydrator. Don't use wax paper because the wax melts.

Dehydrate at 135° for six to eight hours or you may dry at 125° for eight to ten hours with equally good results. Dehydrating times may vary depending on dehydrator model and humidity.

After about five hours, the sauce should be solidified enough for you to peel it off the trays and flip it over for the duration on the drying time. Remove the non-stick sheets during the latter drying stage so both sides of the leather are exposed to the hot air. If you start the drying process before going to bed or work, the leather will turn out fine if you don't flip it. It just may take a little longer to dry and you can always flip and dry it for an hour or so to finish the job when you get to it. The finished product will be leathery and dry to the touch, not sticky.

Allow the leather to cool and then tear it into pieces. Store leather in a jar with a tight fitting lid until you are ready to pack it in plastic bags for a backpacking trip. I have packed sauce leather in mail drops for month-long hikes and it retained its full flavor and quality, although my daily rations were vacuum sealed. Leather which I have stored at home in jars in a cupboard was still in great shape when I ate it after six months. The color turns a little darker over time.

When combined with an equal part of hot water, leather will turn back into tomato sauce.

Salsa Leather

Blend and dry salsa the same way as tomato sauce. Create a tasty Mexican-style meal with rice, chicken and/or black beans, vegetables such as bell peppers and corn, and salsa leather